Heraldic Designs

Royalty-free images of coats-of-arms,
shields, crests, seals, bookplates, and more

Images in this book were drawn from Heraldic
Designs and Engravings for the workshop, Studio and
Library, published in 1913 by J.M. Bergling, and from
American Bookplates by Charles Dexter Allen, pub-
lished by Macmillan and Co. in 1894.

DESIGNER, ENGRAVER
AND PUBLISHER
CHICAGO, U.S.A.

Copyright © 2006 by Schiffer Publishing, Ltd.
Library of Congress Control Number: 2006920025

Designed by Mark David Bowyer
Type set in Berylium and EngrvrsOldEng BT / Aldine721 BT

ISBN: 0-7643-2458-6
Printed in China

Published by Schiffer Publishing Ltd.
4880 Lower Valley Road
Atglen, PA 19310
Phone: (610) 593-1777; Fax: (610) 593-2002
E-mail: Info@schifferbooks.com

For the largest selection of fine reference books on this and related subjects, please visit our web site at **www.schifferbooks.com**
We are always looking for people to write books on new and related subjects. If you have an idea for a book please contact us at the above address.

This book may be purchased from the publisher.
Include $3.95 for shipping.
Please try your bookstore first.
You may write for a free catalog.

In Europe, Schiffer books are distributed by
Bushwood Books
6 Marksbury Ave.
Kew Gardens
Surrey TW9 4JF England
Phone: 44 (0) 20 8392-8585; Fax: 44 (0) 20 8392-9876
E-mail: info@bushwoodbooks.co.uk
Website: www.bushwoodbooks.co.uk
Free postage in the U.K., Europe; air mail at cost.

JOHN M. BERGLING. 1254 ROSEDALE AVE. CHICAGO, U.S.A.

Divisions

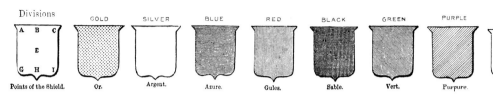

Divisions — Points of the Shield.

A	B	C
	E	
G	H	I

GOLD — Or.

SILVER — Argent.

BLUE — Azure.

RED — Gules.

BLACK — Sable.

GREEN — Vert.

PURPLE — Purpure.

Furs. — Ermine. Vair.

TINCTURES.

Tinctures are represented in engravings and drawings by dots and lines, and those most frequently used in heraldry include two metals, four colors and two furs.

There are a few others but seldom used.

TWO FORMS OF WREATH OR BANDEAU.

It is composed of six twists, may be either curved or straight, and has the same tinctures as the shield and charges, the metal in all cases occupying the first twist on the dexter side.

Divisions of the Shield
into 9 quarters or fields.

A. ____ B.

1.	2.	3.
	10.	
4.	5.	6.
	11.	
7.	8.	9.

C. ____ D.

AB. Upper margin.
CD. Lower margin
AC. Dexter margin.
BD. Sinister margin.
1.2.3. Chief.
4.5.6. Fesse.
7.8.9. Base.
1.4.7. Dexter tierce.
2.5.8. Pale.
3.6.9. Sinister tierce.

1. Dexter chief canton.
2. Chief point.
3. Sinister chief canton.
4. Dexter flank.
5. Centre point.
6. Sinister flank.
7. Dexter canton of base.
8. Base point.
9. Sinister canton of base.
10. Honour point.
11. Nombril point.

One of the several parts denoting the local positions on the escutcheon of any figure or charges.

THE MANTLING,
LAMBREQUIN OR COINTISE.

The ornamental accessories about the helmet and upper part of shield in Armorial Composition. The essential trappings in a complete coat of arms are: 1. the Crest, 2. the Mantling.

SUPPORTERS.

These may consist of mythological figures, men, beasts, birds or fishes. They generally appear in pairs, one on each side of the shield and resting upon the motto scroll. They do not form an essential part of the coat, but rather give an artistic finish to it.

 Pale.

 Bend.

 Fesse.

 Bar.

 Chevron.

 Cross.

 Saltire.

 Paly.

 Bendlet.

 Party per pale.

| A Cross pierced | A Cross voided | A Cross surmounted | Couped and Surmounted Voided | Couped Fimbriated | Cross quartered | Plain Cross Watered | Cross Interlaced | Quarterly Quartered |

 THE FILE or LABEL, Mark of the eldest son.

 THE CRESCENT, The second son's mark.

 THE MULLET, The third son's mark.

 THE MARTLET, The fourth son's mark.

 THE ANNULET, The fifth son's mark

 THE FLEUR-DE-LYS, The sixth son's mark.

 THE ROSE, The seventh son's mark.

 THE CROSS MOLINE, The eighth son's mark.

THE OCTOFOIL, The ninth son's mark.

MARKS OF CADENCY. Distinguishing marks applied to a Coat-of-Arms to indicate the various branches or cadets of a family.

1, Cross of Calvery, a cross on three steps. 2, Latin Cross, a cross the transverse beam of which is placed at one-third the distance from the top of the perpendicular portion, supposed to be the form of cross on which Christ suffered. 3, Tau Cross, (so called from being formed like the Greek letter ⲅ, tau), or cross of St. Anthony, one of the most ancient forms of the cross. 4, Cross of Lorraine. 5, Patriarchal Cross. 6, St. Andrew's Cross, the form of cross on which St. Andrew, the national saint of Scotland, is said to have suffered. 7, Greek Cross, or cross of St. George. the national saint of England, the red cross which appears on British flags. 8, Papal Cross. 9, Cross nowy quadrat, that is, having a square expansion in the center. 10, Maltese Cross, formed of four arrow-heads meeting at the points; the badge of the Knights of Malta. 11, Cross fourchée or forked. 12, Cross pattée or formée. 13, Cross potent or Jerusalem Cross. 14, Cross fleury, from the fleur de lis at its ends.

LINES USED TO DIVIDE THE SHIELD.

- Engrailed
- Invected
- Ondé
- Nebulé
- Indented
- Dancette (3 Indentations)
- Embattled
- Potent
- Raguly
- Dovetailed
- Rayonne
- Nowy
- Escartelé
- Angled
- Bevelled

| Cross Pommetty | Cross Fleury | Quarter'd Fleury | Cross Crossed | Cross Nowey | Cross dearaded | Cross Fusilly | Couped and Fitched | Humetty |

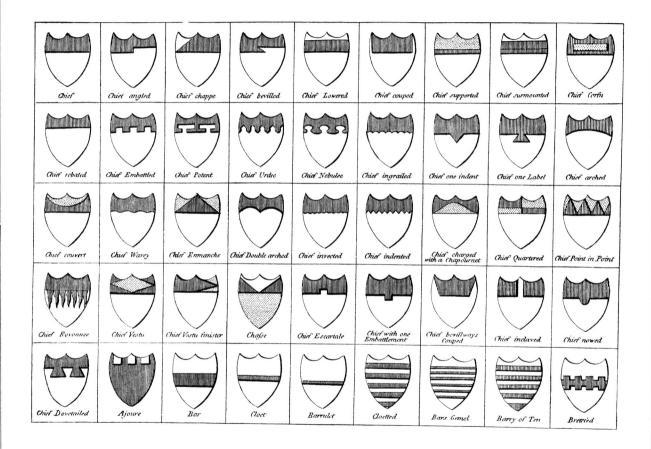

Chief	Chief angled	Chief chappe	Chief bevilled	Chief Lowered	Chief couped	Chief supported	Chief surmounted	Chief Corfu
Chief rebated	Chief Embattled	Chief Potent	Chief Urdee	Chief Nebulee	Chief ingrailed	Chief one indent	Chief one Label	Chief arched
Chief couvert	Chief Wavey	Chief Enmanche	Chief Double arched	Chief invected	Chief indented	Chief charged with a Chapournet	Chief Quartered	Chief Point in Point
Chief Rovonnee	Chief Vestu	Chief Vestu sinister	Chasse	Chief Escartale	Chief with one Embattlement	Chief bevillways Couped	Chief inclaved	Chief nowed
Chief Dovetailed	Ajoure	Bar	Cloet	Barrulet	Cloetted	Bars Gemel	Barry of Ten	Bretted

| Voided and Couped | Cross Potent | Double Fitched | Cross Pomelled | Cross Moline | Cross Mascle at each Point a Plate | Cross Fusil | Triparted Flory | Ansouted |

Partitions and Repartitions of the Shield

| Parted per Bend | Parted per Pale or impaled | Parted per Fess | Parted per Saltier | Parted per Bend Sinister | Parted per Quarter | Parted per Pale Three | Parted Three Fesse | Parted in Three Bendways |

 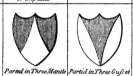   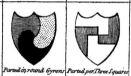

| Parted in Three Bend Sinister | Parted in Three Mantle | Parted in Three Gusset | Parted in Three Traverse Dexter | Parted in Gyron Bend Sinister Ways | Parted in Pale | Parted in round Gyrons | Parted per Three Squares | Parted in Four Gyrons |

| Parted Gyrony of Six | Parted Gyrony of Eight | Parted Champaigne | Parted per Fess per Pale | Parted per Pale in Base | Point Champaigne concav'd | Per Bend Crenelle | Bastile or Embattled | Party per Chev. |

| Cow | Gore | Gusset | Per Pale and Chev | Per Pale and Fess | Paly of Three parted per Fesse | Parted per Pale 1st Quarterly | Parted per Pale and Fess of Six | Paly and Fess of Nine |

Counter Flory	Bronchant	Counter Changed
Abased	Aspersed	Bezanted
Billetty	Checky	Checquer
Braced	Complexed	Cordon
Conjoined	Corded	Banded
Bladed	Aulned	Bottony
Bearded or Blazing	Barbed Dart	Barbed Rose
Canton	Escutcheon	Quarter
A Fret	An Orle	A Pile
Voider	Flasque	Flanch
Treffure	Chaplet	Annulet
Trefoile	Quarterfoile	Cinquefoile
Rostr	Mascle	Lozenge
Fusil	Cap of Maintainance	Cap of State
Aversant	Apaumee	Saliant

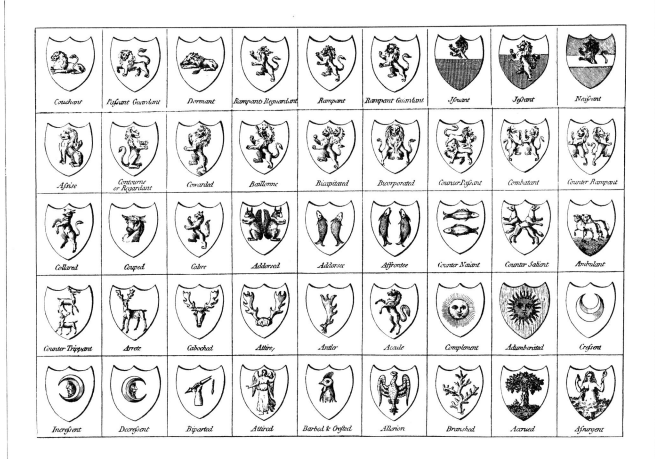

Couchant	Passant Guardant	Dormant	Rampant Reguardant	Rampant	Rampant Guardant	Issuant	Jessant	Naissant
Assise	Contourne or Regardant	Cowarded	Baillonne	Bicapitated	Bicorporated	Counter Passant	Combatant	Counter Rampant
Collared	Couped	Cabre	Addorsed	Addorsee	Affrontee	Counter Naiant	Counter Salient	Ambulant
Counter Trippant	Arrete	Cabocked	Attire,	Antler	Accule	Complement	Adumberated	Cressent
Incressent	Decressent	Biparted	Attired	Barbed & Crested	Allerion	Branshed	Accrued	Assurgent

LE MIEUX QUE JE PUIS

Cheney

Clarence Chapman Cheney

fidelite esr de Dieu

AVISE LA FIN

Alfred C. Kennedy

Sir George Stewart of Grandtully, Bar.ᵗ

INTEGER VITA

AGE OFFICIUM TUUM

J. T. Abbott
Abbeville
Darlington 1866

DIEU ET MON DROIT

James Hatch Esq.

[Illinois]

AUS CHAMBERLAIN.

MORTON

ADDERLEY

HICKMAN

DEUS NOBIS HÆC OTIA FECIT

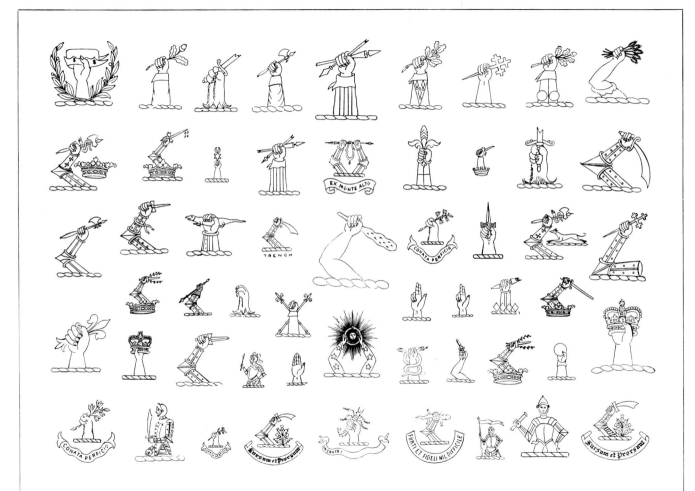

HYDE PARK HOTEL

MITCHELLS & BUTLERS LD
WHITE HORSE HOTEL

DE VERE HOTEL

MIDLAND HOTEL
BIRMINGHAM

BOOTH
QUOD ERO SPERO

TRADE MARK

TOYO KISEN KAISHA

CANADIAN PACIFIC RAILWAY

SPECTEMUR AGENDO
BADAJOZ EGYPT SEVASTOPOL
XXX
CALAMATA INKERMA
CHITRAL

B.C.H.CoLD

PRISCA FIDES

CONSERVATIVE CLUB

PER AD A
AR LT A
DUA ET

GLORIA IN EXCELSIS DEO

BIRMINGHAM RESTAURANT
GWR

WHITE HART HOTEL

COMPAÑIA TRASATLANTICA BARCELONA

FORTITUDE ET FIDELITAS
DUMBARTONSHIRE VOLUNTEERS

29

BARON. BELGIEN.

NOBILITY. SWEDEN.

COUNT. ENGLISH.

MARQUIS. PORTUGAL.

BARON. SWEDISH.

PRINCE OU DUC

ANTIQUE

BARON.

COUNT.

COUNT.

COUNT.

NOBLESSE

MARQUIS

ROYAL. FRANCE.

ROYAL CROWN. PORTUGAL

BONNET DE DIGNITE

PRINCE OF WALES.

ROYAL. SPAIN

VIDAME

IMPERIAL. RUSSIA.

MARQUIS.

COMTE OU VICOMTE

VISCOUNT.

COUNT. SWEDISH

MARQUIS.

BARON

VISCOUNT. ENGLISH.

PATRICIAN. ITALY.

CROWN PRINCE. ITALY.

NOBILITY.

BARON. ENGLISH

UNITED STATES.

K. T.

HOLY BIBLE

G

IN HOC SIGNO VINCES

MASONIC.

33

DEUS MEUMQUE JUS

SCOTTISH RITE.

F.C.B.

KNIGHTS OF PYTHIAS.

F C
B

G

S.K.

R. A.

KSHTW
SSTS

KNIGHTS TEMPLAR

F L T

ODD FELLOWS.

VINCES

32

SPES MEA IN DEO EST

UNIFORMED
PATRIARCHS

ROYAL ARCANUM.

O. OF U. AM. MECHANICS.

A. O. U. WORKMEN.

A. O. U. W.

I. O. FORESTERS

ROYAL LEAGUE.

I. O. OF G. T.

I. O. OF GOOD TEMPLARS.

IND. O. MUT. AID.

WOODMEN.

ANCIENT ORDER OF FORESTERS.

KNIGHTS OF HONOR.

I. O. OF GOOD TEMPLARS.

A. O. OF HIBERNIANS.

I. O. OF RED MEN.

PHI BETA KAPPA

CHI OMEGA

DELTA YPSILON

ZETA PSI

DELTA SIGMA DELTA

CHI PSI

ALPHA CHI OMEGA

SIGMA XI

THETA DELTA CHI

SIGMA CHI

BETA THETA PI

PHI KAPPA PSI

CHI PHI

PI BETA

KAPPA KAPPA GAMMA

ALPHA PHI

PHI DELTA THETA

DELTA GAMMA

ALPHA DELTA PHI

KAPPA SIGMA

ALPHA TAU OMEGA

SIGMA ALPHA EPSILON

DELTA KAPPA EPSILON

DELTA PHI

KAPPA ALPHA

SIGMA NU

PSI UPSILON

PHI GAMMA DELTA

PHI KAPPA SIGMA

41

TROPHIES AND SYMBOLS

42

43

45

HOPE TO SHARE

RIDDELL

FAIBLE SONT FORT VERS NOUS

STEADFAST

SPERO MELIORA

PRO REGE ET REPVBLICA

Lyon King of arms.

MISERERE·MEI·DEVS

CORONET AND SHIELD OF GARTER KING OF ARMS.

TUTUS PROMPTO ANIMO

MANENT OPTIMA CŒLO

SIC VIRESCO

SPES TUTISSIMA CŒLIS

CONCORDIA CRESCIMUS

COPIOSE ET OPPORTUNE

JE VOLL DROIT AVOIR

SPES · BONA

FOR · BEAR

TOVJOVRS PREST

PERIISSEM NI PERIISSEM

TENEBRAS MEAS

Baron Donington.

Wappen gez. von K. Klimsch.

VIRIBUS UNITIS

DUCIT AMOR PATRIÆ

DIEU ME CONDUISE

RATHER DEATHE THAN FALSE OF FAYTHE

Spofford

52

FLORAT QUI LABORAT

WINDSOR CASTLE

WIMBLEDON SURREY S.W.

CREDE CRUCI

HONESTA QUAM MAGNA

SIT DEUS IN STUDIIS

VERITAS NON QUÆRIT ANGULOS

HERIOT of RAMORNIE.

TRUE AND TRUSTY

INTEGRITAS IN PROPOSITO

PAX COPIA

Dum recius sequor

MARGARET NICHOLSON
CORANOUSE CUNINGHAME

EX LIBRIS HENRICI FERRERS FERRERS
MDCCCLXXXIX

Ex Libris
David Francis
Bremner

ERASMVS R AVCH SCHNABE

A LA MODE

SALVO PUDORE

HILLMER

Book Plates Designed and Engraved in

ANTIQUE OR MODERN STYLES

LUCIUS CHARLES COLMAN

EX LIBRIS

VAIRÉ

VAIRÉ

CONTRE-VAIR

SABLE

UXOR
CMNIA
EST ROSA
SUALIS

MAYORQUE

BATAVIA

NUNQUAM NON PARATUS

HAVANE

REPUBLIQUE DOMINICAINE

F. Manning   Needham

Sans ferme

CONFÉDÉRATION ARGENTINE

CHILI

MEXICO

HONDURAS

ROYAUME DE SIAM

GREAT BRITTAIN

FRANCE ROYALE

JAPAN

MOROCCO

HUNGARY

TUNIS

EGYPT

58

VENEZUELA

PERU

EQUADOR

FRENCH EMPIRE

PRUSSIA

DREAD GOD

SAN SALVADOR

MONTEVIDEO

BOLIVIA

BELGIEN

ITALY

GRECI

BRAZIL

HOLLAND

AUSTRIA

NOUVELLE GRENADE

COLOMBIE

ADVERSA VIRTUTE REPELLO

GUATEMALA

NICARAGUA

RUSSIA

PORTUGAL

SWEDEN

TURKEY

DANEMARK

SPAIN

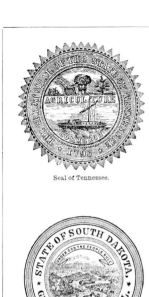

Seal of Tennessee.

Seal of Washington.

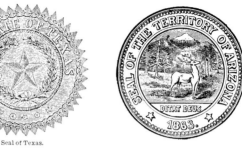

Seal of Texas.

Seal of the Territory of Arizona.

Great seal of South Dakota.

Seal of Kentucky.

Seal of Michigan.

Seal of Maryland.

State seal of Montana.

Seal of New York.

Seal of Utah.

Seal of North Dakota.

Seal of Indiana.

Seal of Louisiana.

Seal of Massachusetts.

Seal of New Hampshire.

Seal of Maine.

Seal of Pennsylvania.

Rhode Island seal

Seal of Minnesota.

Seal of Wyoming.

Seal of Wisconsin.

Seal of North Carolina.

New Jersey.

Connecticut

South Carolina.

Nevada.

Missouri.

New Mexico.

VERMONT

Seal of Iowa.

Seal of Kansas.

Colorado

West Virginia.

Delaware,

Seal of Florida.

Oregon.

Seal of Georgia.

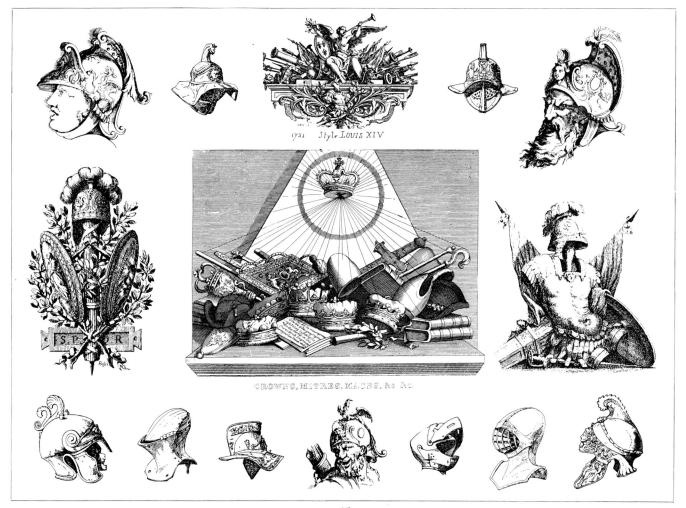

1731 Style LOUIS XIV

CROWNS, MITRES, MACES, &c &c.

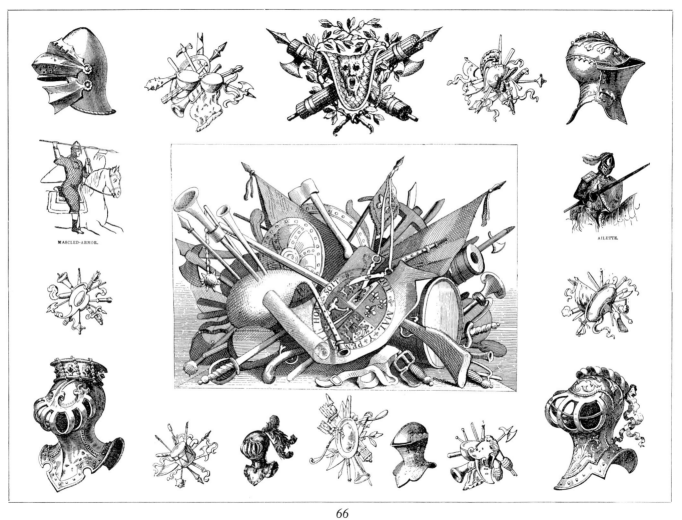

MASCLED-ARMOR.

AILETTE.

MODERN GERMAN GOTHIC

ABCDEFGHIKM
NOPQRSTUVW
abcde XYZ fghikl
mnoprsqtuvwxyz

FRENCH CURSIV

ABCDEFGHI
IJKLMNOPQ
RSTUVWXY

MODERN FRENCH

ABCDEFGHIJKL
MNOPQRSTUW
VXYZ
123456789 &

CHURCH TEXT

ABCDEFGH
IJKLMNOP
QRSTUVW
XYZ

OLD ENGLISH

A few of the most
useful and
Pleasing Alphabets
seen in
Heraldic
and other
Art Designs
Etc.

GERMAN GOTHIC

ABCDEFGHI
KLMNOPQR
STUWXYZ
abcdefghiklm
nopqrstuvw
xyz

GERMAN UNCIAL S·

ABCDEFGHI
JKLMNOPQR
STUVWXYZ
GERMAN 14th Cent.

FRENCH SCRIPT

ABCDEFGHI
JKLMNOPQS
RTCUVWXY

MODERN ROMAN

ABCDEFGHIJKLM
NOPQRSTUVW
abcdef XYZ ghijklm
nopqrstuvxwzy

OMNIA RELINQUIT SERVARE REMPUBLICAM

George Lee Turberville.
Virginia.

Timothy Newell.

I. Thomas, print.

ELIJAH F. REED'S
No. ____ Price ____
A. D. ____

Nocturna versate many versate diurna.

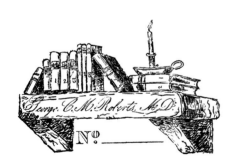

George C. M. Roberts, M. D.

No. ____

Baltimore ____ 18__.

FAMA SED VIRTUS NON MORIATUR

Jared Ingersoll Esq.
of New Haven Connecticut.

FORTIS & FIDUS

PETER MIDDLETON M.D.

LEWIS SC.

John Walters Gibbs, &
Charleston, S? Carolina. —

Dornethie Sculp?

Harrison Gray Otis.

1849

Hannah Reynolds.

RICHARD SPRIGG, jun.

NIL CONSCIRE SIBI

WILLIAM PRESCOTT

Edward Penington

Philadelphia.

Samuel Clam.
Rhode Island

AMICITIAM RETINEBIS ET FIDEM · LIBERTATEM

John Adams.

TREM A LA VERITE

James Eddy Mauran.

Thomas O. Selfridge,

BOSTON,

1799.

Daniel Greenleaf

THE PROPERTY OF

TIMOTHY MANN.

WALPOLE.

Oct.—1810.

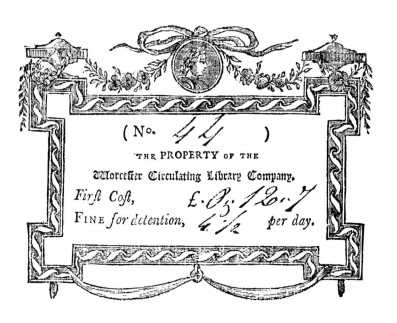

(Nᵒ. 44)

THE PROPERTY OF THE

Worcester Circulating Library Company.

First Cost,   £. 0₃ 12 . 7

FINE *for detention,*   4 ½   per day.

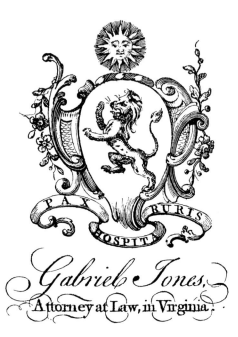

PAX RURIS HOSPIT.

Gabriel Jones,
Attorney at Law, in Virginia.

UN BON LIVRE
EST UN BON
AMI

EX LIBRIS A.L. HOLLINGSWORTH.

ΕΙΣ ΦΑΟΣ

John Durand Esq.

DEUS NOBIS HÆC OTIA FECIT

Thomas Johnston Sculp:

Benj Kissam

PAX QUÆRITUR BELLO

PROSPICERE QUAM ULCISCI

CHRISTI SERVITUS VERA LIBERTAS

Samuel Vaughan Esq.

INDEPENDENCE

POTIORA NON OPTO

EMOLLIT MORES.

NEW-YORK *Society* LIBRARY.

Eng'd by P.R. Maverick 65 Liberty Street.

RESPONDET SEGES VOTIS

1808.
HASTY PUDDING LIBRARY.

Fox

1 $ 33

LINONIAN LIBRARY YALE COLLEGE

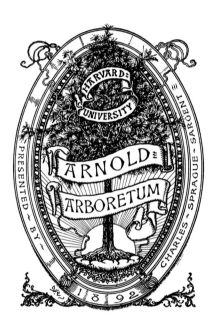

·GIVE ME YOUR FAVOR· MY DULL BRAIN·
·WAS WROUGHT WITH THING...

GEORGE ·ALEXANDER·MACBETH· ·PITTSBURGH·PA·

COLENDO CRESCENT

[ ]

NEC ELA TVS NEC DEJ TVS

three bookplate engravings: a heraldic shield with a tower crest, lions and ladders; a signature "Sam. Hill" within an oval wreath with quill and inkwell; and an ornate cartouche reading "MAY CONCORD PREVAIL AND THE UNDERTAKEING PROSPER" around a central scene, with "ALBANY SOCIETY LIBRARY" and "1759"

Discere Moderatrix Virtutum

Josiah Quincy

ASHMEAD
WILLIAM
WHITMELL
CHARLESTON S.C.

John Quincy Adams.

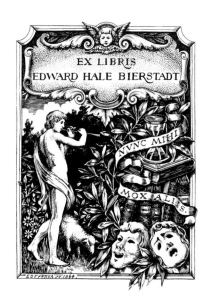

EX LIBRIS
EDWARD HALE BIERSTADT

NVNC MIHI

MOX ALIIS.

EXITUS ACTA PROBAT

Bushrod Washington

EXITUS ACTA PROBAT

George Washington

PER AMPLIORA AD ALTIORA

Oliver Wendell Holmes.

VERA PRO GRATIS

David Webster

Winfield Scott.

John Chandler Jun.ʳ Esq.ʳ

N. Hurd Sculp

Robert Hale Esq.ʳ
OF BEVERLY

N. Hurd Sc.ᵗ

Lewⁱˢ DeBlois

N. Hurd Sculp

FOLLOW·REASON

Joshua Spooner.

N·Hurd Sc.ᵗ

N Hurd Sculp

N.º   [   ]

OCCASIONEM COGNOSCE

APPRENTICES' LIBRARY.

A. Anderson Sc.

Presented by

Peter A. Browne

Engraved by James D. Akin.

SUB LIBERTATE FLORENT

AMERICAN ACADEMY OF ARTS & SCIENCES.

V. D. C. C. L X X X.

The GIFT of

George Goodwin

N.º

DICTIS FACTISQUE SIMPLEX

HENRY D. GILPIN.

Whitehead Hicks, Esq.

H. DAWKINS, Sculp.

Eli Forbes.

J. M. Furnass Sc.

John Chambers Esq.r
E. Gallaudet
Sculp.

WASTE NOT A MOMENT

Social Library
Stepney Society
WETHERSFIELD

Nᵒ 215

Doolittle Sculp.

HONORATUS QUI VIRTUTEM
HONORAT

EDMUND·H·
GARRETT

INSTAVRATIO·SALVTIS·PVBLICAE

Nº   [ ]

Gardiner Chandler

Abraham Bancker

Weigh well each thought, each sentence freely scan,
In Reason's balance try the works of man:
Be bias'd not by those who praise or blame,
Nor, servile, Yield opinion to a Name.

William Wetmore

Paul Revere

PRO·ARIS ET·FOCIS

Bloomfield

Maingot del.^t   Maverick Sc.^t

Maverick Sc.

UTERE MUNDO.

Absalom Blachly.

T. F. Barralet invt.   *J. H. Seymour sc*

Bloomfield McIlvaine.

Colonel John Skey Eustace, State of New York.

SANS DIEU RIEN

Ignotis errare locis, ignota videre,
Flumina gaudebat: studio minuente laborem.

TOVIOVRS · PREST

THE · HONOURABLE
Wᴹ · CARMICHAELL
ESQᴿ

PROCURATA INDUSTRIA

Andrew G. Fraunces.

AUDACITER

J.H. Ewing

John Goelet

Barrak Hays

Samuel Farmar Jarvis. D.D.

William Jauncey

Richard Harison Esq.

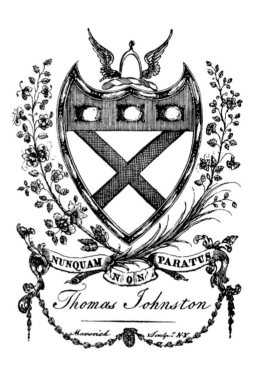

Thomas Johnston

Francis Panton Jun.ᵣ

MORI QUAM FŒDARI
MALO VIRTUTI

IUNCTA FIDES

THE REV.ᴰ IOHN MURRAY.

DUM·CLAVUM·TENEAM

William Penn Esq.r Proprietor of Pensylvania ;1703

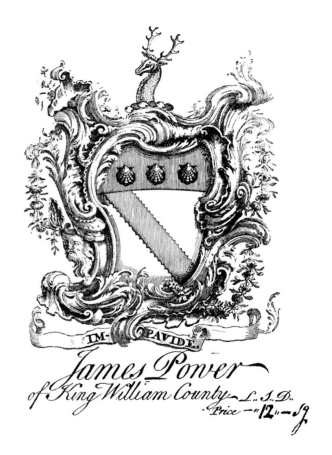

IM-·PAVIDE

James Power of King William County. L. S. D.

Price — "12" — S 9

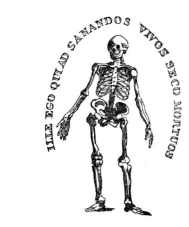

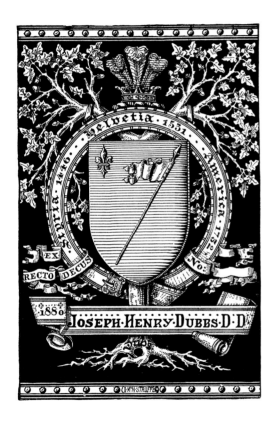

George H. Ellwanger.

LE DIABLE

COURAGE

EST MORT

SAMUEL·WESLEY·MARVIN

EX LIBRIS ~ JULIA DEXTER COFFIN

Bailey

Thomas

Aldrich

His Mark

Virginia Council Chamber.

Arthur Robinson Stone

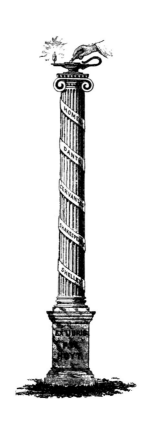